Minimizing Personal Stress

Minimizar el estrés Personal

Bilingual in English and Spanish

Carmen S. Gonzalez, MS.Ed.

Introduction:

Imagine living in an environment where one were under stress all the time, yet they must deal with it alone. There is no one that can connect with you on a personal level that can help you so it leaves one to resort to other means. At times, these means may affect your personal life and domino into your work environment.

Are you in a situation for the sake of convenience in any of these areas?

A. Work in a place that makes you feel uncomfortable

B. Relationship with an energy vampire

C. Living Circumstances

D. All of the Above.

If you have chosen any of these circumstances then you have come to the right place. In this book, you will learn strategies for these areas that can affect your stress levels. It will be a quick resource that will get to the point.

Work and Stress

Many people choose a job, because of the convenience. Some people enjoy it in the beginning and find that it does not have the same fulfillment with time. When this happens then we need to rewire our thinking. There are some things that we can do on the job to minimize work-related stress.

Allow for more flexibility on the job. Come into your job early, and do what you need to do to prepare for your day. If you are a subcontractor then you may want to start your day on the job 30 minutes earlier, and wake up a couple of hours early.

Ignore negative talk, by trying positive self-talk. Stand in front of

the mirror and look at your eyes. Say
something positive about yourself for
about 5 minutes. This will help your
serotonin levels and reduce depression.

Self-talk and positive
affirmations can also reduce anxiety,
by giving you more confidence and
reducing the fight or flight response.
You will want to fight for your self-
confidence to be boosted internally.
More than likely drinking alcoholic
beverages, street drugs, and other bad
habits will be eliminated.

On the job is important to work at
your own pace. Do you often feel
rushed on the job? Many people with
this predicament often do well when
they put themselves on a schedule for

time management. Spread your work out across time, but prioritize what needs to be done first. Come into work mentally prepared to work and prevent poor performance.

Some people benefit from frequent breaks. It does not have to look like a break, but if you need a break then say something. Communicate your needs are take an exercise or water break during the day to keep yourself going.

If you must take medicine for any reason, no matter what it is for, make sure that you remain compliant. This will reduce problems in the future. Be sure to have a meal with your medicine. Stress from your brain goes to your brain. The combination of stress and no food in your stomach when you should be taking medicine will not benefit you in the long run.

Avoid heat and excessive sun when you are stressed out. You may need to stay in a shaded area or cooler area if it is too hot outdoors. By exposing yourself to too much heat and sun, you may be at risk to even more heat exhaustion, especially on certain medicines. In turn, you may have nausea or even a tension headache, which feels uncomfortable.

When all else fails, learn to adapt to your job. You can learn a shortcut. You can even learn a new job with your current employer.

Take into consideration that everyone has a different work style. Learn the needs of your employer. Stay on good terms, by being persistent. Do not give up on your dream. If it appears too hard in the beginning, no job is easy, look at the reward at the end of the tunnel.

Energy Vampires and Stress

Energy vampires are just like those you see in horror films, although not sucking up all your blood, but it sure feels like it. The suck up all your energy and by the time you finish talking to these individuals, you are tired. They are individuals that are needy without a cause.

Energy vampires are self-absorbed individuals that have so many problems that they do not let you have your own life back. They are ambivalent in nature, because they cling to you like a leech. They are not friends that

will listen to you, they are those that
you want to avoid.

When you are around an energy
vampire, you will not know immediately.
It will take some time, to know that
they are energy vampires. They do not
have a real hobby. They usually just
want to either absorb all of you or
your resources, until you have nothing
left.

I can remember an individual being
confronted about a situation at work.
I then witnessed the individual look
tired and it was break time, but she
could not get away. It was frigidly
cold outdoors. If it were me, I would
have started taking break outside,
during cold or warm weather.

Otherwise, why call it a break if you are going to be drained by energy vampires during break. Spend that time talking to those that you love, and enjoy a meal/healthy beverage.

At times, there is no getting away from these energy vampires. You may discover that these energy vampires are like stalkers. At this point, you may have to block the phone number. You may even have to resort to not letting the individual know where you live to keep your privacy. If they find out where you live, do not open your door if they were not invited.

Do not accept energy vampire food. Food that is offered by an energy vampire is merely a trap. They offer the food as a form of getting closer to you, whether it taste good or terrible. Do not try it, or you will be stuck there eating and absorbing all their negative energy.

The polite way to treat an energy vampire is to just say no thank you. An explanation is not needed. If they require an explanation, just say that you will get back to them later, because you need a break. Then politely excuse yourself.

Energy vampires increase stress levels. If you are feeling depressed, you may become more depressed. If you have anxiety, then you may increase anxiety. All problems will appear to be magnified.

Unwanted Callers and stress

We have probably all been a
witness or victim of the unwanted

callers. Unwanted callers raise our stress levels, because it can cause physical ailments to occur. Serotonin levels may become disrupted, due to energy dropping.

This is when one must resort to blocking the caller permanently. Do not wait until the lewd photos come in, causing you problems in your relationship. Do not wait until the individual finds out where you live with an internet search. By this time, you will probably be too late.

Unwanted callers are doing this to hurt you or your relationship. They may send inappropriate data to disrupt your current relationship. Where you may love your current individual or loved one, you may hurt this special someone with calls from this individual. This may start a string of fights or a bad fight without any filters. Handle the situation fast, if you really love your current relationship. Calling your provider to block the number counts just as much. Cut off all ties as quickly as possible.

Do not attempt to rekindle anything for fear that you may upset them. This is not love. This is being a pure stalker. If they begin to stalk your family, then this is a problem. You may have to lose contact with them too, because they are trying to be hilarious when it is pure

vindictiveness and malice.

Living Circumstances and Stress

Where we live can affect our stress levels. If you are living an area where there is a lot of negative activity outdoors, then realize that you can always stay indoors. At times, this is the best alternative. It keeps us away from problems.

However, if you are in a living situation where you have an apartment,

yet the landlord refuses repairs or
extermination of pest, then you have a
problem. At times, people fall victim
and stay living in slum lord home.
People then do things here and there
that can escalate like making it take a
toll on our personal life.

Eventually, you may not want to
invite anyone over to your home,
because it feels embarrassing. At
times, something drastic must happen
before you say enough is enough. Then
you finally call rent control.

The most important thing to do is
to do a thorough cleansing of your
home. You want to eliminate anything
that can increase your stress levels.
You may also want to add your favorite

scent to your home, to help you bring in positive vibrations.

You may want to decorate your home with brighter colors. For a lot of women, it may be difficulty due to personal reasons. When this becomes a problem then try lighter colors for your curtains instead.

Try to make your home the way that you want it to look. You do not have to be a millionaire to make your home feel like a millionaire home. Make it look the way you have always envisioned your home to look.

Minimizar el estrés Personal

Carmen S. Gonzalez, MS.Ed.

Introducción:

Imagina vivir en un ambiente donde uno estaba bajo estrés todo el tiempo, sin embargo, debe lidiar con él solo. No hay nadie que pueda conectarse con usted a nivel personal que puede ayudarle por lo que deja uno para recurrir a otros medios. A veces, estos medios pueden afectar su vida personal y domino en su entorno de trabajo.

¿Estás en una situación por conveniencia en cualquiera de estas áreas?

A. Trabajar en un lugar que te hace sentir incómodo

B. Relación con un vampiro de energía

C. Viviendo circunstancias

D. Todo.

Si ha elegido alguna de estas circunstancias han llegado al lugar correcto. En este libro, usted aprenderá estrategias para estas áreas que pueden afectar sus niveles de estrés. Va a ser un recurso rápido que llega al punto.

Trabajo y el estrés

Muchas personas eligen un trabajo, debido a la comodidad. Algunas personas disfrutan en principio y encuentran que no tiene el mismo cumplimiento con el tiempo. Cuando esto sucede tenemos que recablear de nuestro pensamiento. Hay algunas cosas que podemos hacer en el trabajo para minimizar el estrés laboral.

Permiten más flexibilidad en el trabajo. En su trabajo temprano y qué necesita hacer para prepararse para su día. Si usted es un subcontratista puede comenzar su día en el trabajo 30 minutos antes, y despertar un par de horas temprano.

Ignore la charla negativa, intentando positivo dialogo. Parado frente al espejo y mirar a los ojos. Decir algo positivo sobre ti mismo durante unos 5 minutos. Esto ayudará a tus niveles de serotonina y reducir la depresión.

Dialogo y positivas afirmaciones también pueden reducir la ansiedad, que le da más confianza y reduciendo la respuesta de lucha o huida. Tienes que luchar por su confianza en sí mismo ser impulsado internamente. Más que probable que beber bebidas alcohólicas, drogas de la calle, y otros malos hábitos serán eliminados.

En el trabajo es importante trabajar a su propio ritmo. ¿A menudo sientes apurado en el trabajo? Muchas personas con esta situación a menudo hacen bien cuando se ponen en un programa de gestión del tiempo. Extendió su trabajo a través del tiempo, pero priorizamos lo que hay que hacer primero. Entra en trabajo preparado mentalmente para trabajar y evitar malos resultados.

Algunas personas se benefician de descansos frecuentes. No tiene que parecerse a un descanso, pero si usted necesita un descanso y luego decir algo. Comunicar que sus necesidades son tomar un descanso del ejercicio o agua durante el día para mantenerte yendo.

Si debe tomar medicina por cualquier motivo, no importa lo que sea, asegúrese de que usted siendo obediente. Esto reduce problemas en el futuro. Asegúrese de tener una comida con su medicina. Estrés de su cerebro va a tu cerebro. La combinación de estrés y no hay comida en el estómago cuando se debe tomar medicina no beneficiará a largo plazo.

Evite el calor y el sol excesivo cuando están estresados. Usted puede necesitar permanecer en un área sombreada o un área más fresca si es demasiado caliente al aire libre. Exponiendo a ti mismo a demasiado calor y el sol, puede estar en riesgo de agotamiento por calor aún más, sobre todo en ciertos medicamentos. A su vez puede tener náuseas o incluso una cefalea tensional, que se siente incómoda.

Cuando todo lo demás falla, aprender a adaptarse a su trabajo. Puede obtener un acceso directo. Incluso puede aprender un nuevo trabajo con su empleador actual.

Tener en cuenta que cada uno tiene un estilo de trabajo diferente. Conocer las necesidades de su empleador. Mantenerse en buenos términos, por ser persistente. No desistas en tu sueño. Si parece demasiado difícil al principio, no hay trabajo es fácil, mira la recompensa al final del túnel.

Estrés y vampiros de energía

Vampiros de energía son como las ves en películas de horror, aunque no succionar toda la sangre, pero que se siente como él. La chupan toda tu energía y cuando que termine de hablar con estas personas, estás cansado. Son personas que están necesitadas sin una causa.

Vampiros de energía son individuos egocéntrica que tienen tantos problemas que no te permiten tener tu propia vida detrás. Son ambivalentes en la naturaleza, porque se aferran a usted como una sanguijuela. No son amigos que se escuchan, son los que quiere evitar.

Cuando usted está alrededor de un vampiro de energía, no sabrás inmediatamente. Tomará algún tiempo, saber que ellos son vampiros de energía. No tienen un verdadero hobby. Generalmente solo quieren tampoco absorber todo de usted o de sus recursos, hasta que no tiene nada.

Recuerdo a un individuo que se enfrentó a una situación en el trabajo. Entonces presencié la mirada individual cansada y era tiempo de descanso, pero ella no podía escapar. Fue frigider frio al aire libre. Si se tratara de mí, habría empecé a tomar el descanso afuera, durante el tiempo frío o caliente. De lo contrario, por qué lo llaman un descanso si vas a drenar por los vampiros de energía durante las vacaciones. Pasar ese tiempo hablando con los que amas y disfrutar de una comida/saludable bebida.

A veces, no hay alejarse de estos vampiros de energía. Usted puede descubrir que estos vampiros de energía son como acosadores. En este punto, usted puede tener que bloquear el número de teléfono. Incluso puede tener que recurrir a no dejar que el individuo sabe dónde vives para mantener su privacidad. Si se dan cuenta donde vives, no abra la puerta si no fueron invitados.

No se aceptan alimentos de energía Vampiro. La comida que se ofrece por un vampiro de energía es simplemente una trampa. Ofrecen la comida como una forma de acercarse a usted, si gusto bueno o terrible. No intentarlo, o va a ser atrapado ahí comiendo y absorbiendo toda su energía negativa.

La forma educada para tratar a un vampiro de energía es no decir gracias. No es necesaria una explicación. Si requiere una explicación, digamos que va a volver a ellas más tarde, porque usted necesita un descanso. Luego cortésmente excusa a sí mismo.

Vampiros de energía aumentan los niveles de estrés. Si usted se siente deprimido, usted puede deprimirse más.

Si tiene ansiedad, puede aumentar
ansiedad. Todoslos problemas parece
magnificarse.

Llamadas no deseadas y el estrés

Probablemente todos hemos sido un testigo o víctima de las llamadas no deseadas. No deseadas que llaman elevar nuestros niveles de estrés, porque puede causar dolencias físicas que se produzcan. Los niveles de serotonina pueden ser interrumpidos debido a la caída de energía.

Esto es cuando se debe recurrir a bloquear la persona que llama permanentemente. No espere hasta que las fotos lascivas, causando problemas en tu relación. No espere hasta que el individuo se entera de donde usted vive con una búsqueda en internet. Por este tiempo, usted probablemente será demasiado tarde.

Llamadas no deseadas están haciendo esto para lesionarlo a usted o a su relación. Pueden enviar datos inadecuados para interrumpir su relación actual. Donde usted puede amar a su persona actual o ser querido, usted puede lastimar a este especial alguien con llamadas de esta persona. Éste puede iniciar una cadena de luchas o una mala lucha sin filtros. Manejar la situación rápidamente, si realmente amas a tu actual relación. Llamar a su proveedor para bloquear las cuentas número igual. Cortar todos los lazos lo antes posible.

No trate de dar vida a nada por miedo a que puede alterarlos. Esto no es amor. Esto es ser un acosador puro. Si

empiezan a acechar a su familia, este
es un problema. Usted puede tener
perder el contacto con ellos, porque
están tratando de ser desternillante
cuando es pura venganza y malicia.

Estrés y las circunstancias de la vida

Donde vivimos pueden afectar nuestros niveles de estrés. Si usted está viviendo en una zona donde hay un montón de negativos de la actividad al aire libre, entonces se dan cuenta que siempre puede permanecer en el interior. A veces, esta es la mejor alternativa. Nos mantiene lejos de problemas.

Sin embargo, si usted está en una situación de vida que tiene un piso, pero el propietario niega a reparaciones o exterminación de plagas, entonces usted tiene un problema. A veces, gente víctima y permanecer viviendo en casa de Señor de tugurios. La gente entonces hacer cosas aquí y allá que pueden escalar como lo que es tomar un peaje en nuestra vida personal.

Finalmente, no puede invitar a alguien más a su casa, porque siente vergüenza. A veces, algo drástico debe ocurrir antes que decir basta ya. Entonces finalmente llamada control de alquileres.

Lo más importante es hacer una limpieza completa de su hogar. Quiere todo lo que puede aumentar sus niveles de estrés eliminar. También puedes añadir tu aroma favorito a su casa, para ayudar a traer en vibraciones positivas.

Puedes decorar tu hogar con colores más brillantes. Para muchas mujeres, puede ser dificultad debido a motivos personales. Cuando esto se convierte en un problema intente colores más claros para sus cortinas en su lugar.

Trate de hacer su hogar lo que usted quisiera que mirara. No tienes que ser millonario para hacer tu casa se sienta

como en casa de un millonario. Que se
vea la manera que usted siempre ha
imaginado su casa para ver.

.

A Little Book of Positive Affirmations

Carmen S. Gonzalez

Dear God,

Allow me to be able to say the
right thing at the right time to
attract monetary wealth.   I know that
I can make it rich in life. Help me to
attract money and grow richer.

Day # 1   Affirmation of Monetary
Wealth

Money does not go on trees, but I know
that I a capable of earning up to my
full potential. I am worthy of being
wealthy and successful in all aspects
of my life. I can become beyond a
hundredaire, thousand Aire, and even a
millionaire, because I am a monetary
genius.

    I am rich. I have great ideas. I
have a unique entrepreneurial spirit.
I have ideas that will last a lifetime.
I have great ideas. I am investable.

    I am wealthy. I am full of
monetary potential. I am full of
usefulness and I will excel in my
craft. Money is not worth much unless

you spread it around, but I can spread
it as far as the Earth can carry it.
I am a money-making machine.

I am full of monetary wealth. I
make my income the legitimate way. My
ideas have no ends. I can make it as
far as possible if I remain focused. I
can fund my company, work ideas, or
projects.

I am a monetary self- starter.
Once I start making money, I do not
stop. I can carry myself through any
situation involving my funds. My funds
only travel through good experiences
that involve a positive atmosphere.

I am full of monetary wealth. I
make conscious decisions with my money.

I can buy myself what I wish to buy and enjoy my life.

I am worthy of being wealthy. I will not feel guilty about my full financial potential. I will never liquidate all my funds. I know how to budget accordingly.

Health...

Dear God,

Great health is something that I can achieve. Come into my life and allow me to have great health with this

plan. Heal me, help me, and allow me

to succeed in reaching this goal.

Day # 2

Affirmation of Health

They say that an apple a day can

save me.   I am healthy, I have a

healthy B.M.I. I make great decisions

when it comes to my diet.   I am

completely hydrated with the proper

amounts of water.

I am fully in great health. I

always stay in great health.   I

exercise regularly. I have the proper

amounts of vitamin D in my body. I get
enough sunlight.

I am fully rested with the proper
amount of sleep. I take naps when
necessary. I am not over-worked or
tired, because my Melatonin needs to
build up for cell repair and I know
this.

I am in excellent health. I have
an exercise regimen from head to toe.
I am aware that I need to continue to
move to reach my goals in terms of my
head to toe health and remain
proactive.

I am aware that going to the
doctor is necessary and I am already
doing this. I visit my doctor
regularly for all ailments to ensure

that I am doing fine as a confirmation. I have completed all necessary tests for preventative care. I am doing just fine, because there are no more surprises.

I am always staying in great health. I am fully aware that I will continue to follow best practices by getting professional advice for my ailments that need help. In general, I am fully healthy with a great diet, sleep, exercise, and overall regimen.

Self- Love…

Dear God,

Help me to love myself once again with these words. Allow me to project self-love in positive direction. I thank you for opening my eyes tc realize that it is possible, for self-love is something attainable.

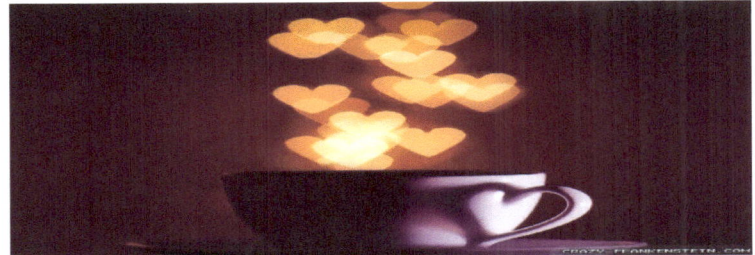

Day # 3   Affirmation of Self-Love

I am worthy of loving myself. I love everything about myself. I am uniquely loveable. I am like no one else.

I love myself. I am wonderful. I am an excellent individual. I am creative in my own right.

I love myself. I am worthy of great things. I always project self-love. This love transcends into all that I do. I also attract positive people and things in my life.

I am lovable and I am loving everything about myself. I might not be perfect, but I love that I acknowledge my great qualities every day.

List your great qualities...

#1 _____

#2_____

#3_____

These qualities I would never trade for anything in the world.

My self-love is imperative to all that I do and all that I am. I am compassionate, caring, and charismatic. I am patient, passive, and pure at heart. I am reliable, reserved, and ready to take on new challenges. I do this all with my self- love, because I can.

I am capable of being my own best friend. I can love myself more than anyone else can. To love myself is something that I will always treasure. I love myself, because this is God's greatest gift that I can ever attain.

Day #4   Affirmation of Self-Worth

I am worth more than money can buy. I am a luxury item that is irreplaceable. I am worthy of all self-worth that climbs beyond what money can buy.

I would never put a price on myself, but if I had to, I deserve the best that money can offer. As I look in the mirror I see an individual that is respected and highly reputable. I am career wise very successful, because I know that I deserve the best.

I will not make myself available just for the sake of it, to those who do not deserve my presence for they are social vampires. I will eradicate every social vampire by completely ignoring them when they are in my presence. I will eliminate all that attempt to diminish my self-worth by ignoring petty gossip and immature clinginess.

I will continue to illuminate a sense of positive self-worth in my life by projecting this as an essence of who I am. I am a positively mature, distinguished, and avid illuminator of positive light and likeness. I am a blessed individual that is going to keep all the blessings coming in by continuing to block all negativity, by surrounding myself with likeminded energy always.

I am a self- motivated individual that will continue to encourage positive self- worth that is inspiring, intelligent, and bright. As this individual, I will continue to bring about positive social change. I have the power to influence my own future by bringing to presence my own heightened sense of self-worth that is powerful yet God fearing.

Day # 5   Affirmation of Brilliance

I am brilliant. I am an innovator that can bring about social change with just my thoughts. I am studious and analytical. I am creative and put my knowledge to excellent use.

I am as Brilliant as the father of Medicine, because I oversee my own oath now, and I am taking charge. I am so

Brilliant that I am a brilliant theorist. I have no classification, which makes me even better at what I do.

I am a brilliant artist, writer, and entertainer of individuals. Although I have an exact career, I am what I make of it. My costumes that I choose are uniforms that I created with a purpose every day. They keep me in character.

I am a Brilliant individual to my family members and loved ones. I am a brilliant example of a shining star that will not stop blinging and blinking. I am a brilliant innovator of works.

Day #6   Affirmation of Inner

Beauty

    I am beautiful on the inside. I

project my beauty outwardly with a

social charity of inner beauty

management. I am a beautiful creature

by nature that is a force that will not

be eliminated.

    My inner beauty is loved by all

humanity. It is especially loved by my

_____. My inner beauty is

especially loved by me and my family.

    My inner beauty is so fierce that

I need my own runway to display it. My

inner beauty is like a type of rare

couture. My inner beauty is like a rare diamond topaz that must be lab created to be replicated.

My inner beauty is a song that will never go wrong. It is a love song that has yet to be created, for a me that will never go away. My inner beauty is a sense of peace that will never be reconciled for another.

My _____will need to earn me through my inner beauty first. Now, I will accept another in my world by accepting me first. My inner beauty is unique, fierce, and loved by all. I do

accept myself despite a traditional
proposal from my _____.

Day #7   Affirmation of Inner
Talents

     I am talented. I am beyond a
triple threat with my talent, because
it is inspired by God. I have unique
talents that will not be taken away. I
am a talent that can make extreme
amounts of riches in my life.

     I am a songstress that can convert
poetry and stories into genuine art.
I am a writer that can create beautiful
work that is powerful and to the point.
I am whatever I want to be and I am
excellent at it, despite what others

may think I was given this talent to
enjoy my life and make money with it.

I am a _____, doctor, a
teacher, an educator, a great
therapist. Others come to me for help,
and I can fix it. People trust in my
judgement as a professional, because I
can give great advice without any
hesitation.

I am a talented and creative
member of my society, because I keep
the economy productive. My business is
unique, because it entails all my
talents at one time to help the
youngest generation. I spend my money
wisely on things pertaining to my
talents involving my business.

I am multi-talented. I am a
multi-linguist. I am extremely
multicultural in the fact that I pick
up new variations to my talent.

Day #8 Affirmation of Piety

I am a God-fearing individual.
When I feel neglected, I know that God
will never stop loving me. I know that
God will continue to take care of me,
even when my love from others has
failed. I am a pious, God revering
individual that will sow my seeds to
God with my talents. I give my love to
God by spreading my love to humanity
through good works.

Day # 9 Affirmation of Credibility

I believe in my ability to reach my goals. I believe in myself to be able to become extremely rich. I believe in my goals of making my business ordeals successful. I believe that I can and will bring about change with trust in God.

I believe that I will be able to purchase things that make sense in my budget that can and will last a lifetime. I believe that I will make a great parent to my children. I believe that my children will follow in my footsteps. I believe that the choices that I make today will impact my future, and that I am making the correct decisions.

#1 _____

#2_____

#3 _____

Day # 10 Affirmation of Power

I am a powerful individual that
continues to empower myself through
self-reflection. I have a power over
my future, because I take charge. I
have the power to multiply my funds in
another business venture. I will open
another business that involves having a
store once I am able to save around my
goal income.

I have the power and self
determination to remain focused and
make my dreams come true. I have the
power to finally become where I want to
be in terms of my relationship. I have

the power to become free in terms of my thinking.

I have the power to have strong will power. I have the power to be self-sufficient and independent. I have the power to make it with any venture that I choose without quitting or getting let go from my business ideas. I have the power to not self-destruct.

I have the power to be constructive in anything that I choose to do. I have the power to make the best decisions. I have the power to make as much as I would like to make and to grow each month and not diminish my self-worth. I have the power to live with dignity.

Day # 11 Affirmation of Creativity

I am creative. I am a talented creative engineer of thought. I can influence the future to follow ny way of thinking and to continue to be supportive until they too can grow rich and strong and continue to be inspired by me.

I am a creative engineer of professional writing. I can make money from my talent. I can continue to invest in my work as an author.

I am a creatively talented individual that is loved by all. People admire my work as an artist. I am great at what I do as a creative individual.

Day #12 Affirmation of Genuine Gift

I believe that I have a genuine gift.
I believe that it comes from God. I
believe that my genuine gift is to
teach and heal the disabled. I believe
that I have a gift that is rare that
cannot be contended with.

Day #13 Affirmation of Sweetness

I am sweet. I am like sugar and spice.
I can erase all sad events and make
individuals that I love feel better.

I am sweet. I am like cinnamon and
sugar. I add to all events by
spreading joy.

I am sweet. I am neat and sweet like a
sugar cane juice. I can make your day
complete.

I am sweet. I do not hurt. I am a sweet sensation once you get to know me at an instant.

Day #14 Affirmation of Intellectual Genius

I am an individual that is an intellectual genius. My ideas are one of a kind. I am an intellectual genius that will continue to grow even more intelligent every day.

I am an intellectual genius that will continue to be inspired by the first pioneers that have inspired me from the beginning. I will continue to develop my ideas until they are fully created. I am an intellectual genius that will encourage others to not give up on their intelligence as I grow my own for the sake of the greater good.

Day #15 Affirmation of Personal Growth

I am capable of personal growth. I am not a product of the Establishment. I am a product of a higher power with a Grand Plan.

I can grow in my personal endeavors...

#1 _____

#2 _____

#3 _____

I will achieve them by any means necessary, because I can grow in this direction with perseverance and determination.

Day #16 Affirmation of Strength

I am strong mentally, physically, and emotionally. At times, I am aware that I do not know my own strength. My strength can move mountains.

I am one that can challenge theory that can be improved upon. I am an engineer of my own strength. In my eyes, there is always room to grow.

I am strong spiritually. I will continue to always meditate in my heart. I will continue to believe in God's word when all else seems to not work, because he keeps me strong.

Day#17 Affirmation of Positive Energy

I surround myself with positive energy. This energy never gives up on me. My aura is completely positive.

I rebuke negative energy by erasing all negativity from my life by asking God to remove this negative energy. God is the captain of my positive energy, but it is up to me to accept it.   I will continue to be driven by only positive energy for now and forever.

Day #18 Affirmation of Acceptance of a Condition

I am aware that everyone has a condition that they must deal with or we would not be human. Although I accept the condition of

_____, because

of a medical diagnosis, I am aware that

I do not have to remain on the disabled

list. I remove the stigma behind

_____ (the condition), by

continuing to live my life the best

that I possibly can.

Day#19 Affirmation of Advanced

Capabilities

    I can advance all my capabilities

with my talents by using a combination

of common sense and research. I will

continue to encourage myself to grow by

continuing to work on my craft. I will

continue to use common sense to make

the correct decisions so that my mind

will not diminish in intelligence.

Day#20 Affirmation to Beat All Odds

I am not a product of my environment or the establishment. I will continue to beat all odds by not returning to the situation that caused mayhem in my life. I will achieve this by beating all odds and surrounding myself with only positive energy.

I will use my talents for the greater good. I will beat all odds and begin to change for the better.

#1 Where I am....

_____

_____

_____

_____

_____

#2 Where I want to be...

_____

_____

_____

_____

_____

#3 How I will get there?

_____

_____

_____

_____

_____

Day#21 Affirmation of Acceptance of

Self-Image

I am a gorgeous individual. I love how my eyes sparkle with innocence. I love how my nose is so distinct and full of character. I love how my ears are sensitive to beautiful melodies and sweet words. I love how my skin shines with my favorite oils. I love my pheromones/scent and how they attract my _____, when I apply my favorite spray to heighten my pheromones.   I love my unique features, because they make me who I am _____(state what they are).

I love that I have the unique ability to look different and project myself as an individual that is full of character. I love me.

Day #22 I am Strong

I am strong. I am a product of a productive environment that I helped to build. I am an expert in the art of building a strong subconscious mind. I am strong and focused. I am full of good-faith and amazing work ethic. I believe in me. Faith is important to me.

Day # 23 I can take care of me…

All I need is me. At the end, all I have is myself to lean on. I can carry myself with respect and dignity. I am like an ox. I can fend for myself. I am as wise an owl. I know how to maneuver in any environment.

Day #24 I am of good faith...

I am a law-abiding citizen. I do not break the law. I am not a product of my environment. I will not be devoured by vultures. I am full of integrity. I know how to remove myself from a situation before it escalates. Nothing is too big of a task when it comes to doing the right thing at the right time. I follow the rules, even when those around me are in disarray.

Day #25 I am in Control...

I am in control of my own destiny. I have control over what goes right in my life. I am in control of my life and finances. I am in control of how I want to look. I am in control of my habitat and my living space no matter where I am.

Day #26 I am at Peace…

My mind is at peace. My soul is at peace. I am so peace, and I have zero worries. I am at peace with myself, and my peace is so soothing.

Day #27   I am Happy…

I am so happy that it is contagious. Those who do not know me welcome me with open arms. My happiness rolls over into all areas of my life.

Day #28   I am Successful...

I take every day one day at a time. I am successful no matter where I am in my life. I am a successful individual that can make any circumstance look easy to beat and win.

Day #29   I am Great ...

I am great at all that I do. I am great at all that I learn that is new. I am a great expert in my field. I am a great individual overall.

Day #30   I am a Winner...

I am a winner. I am a trophy. I am a star in all that I do. I am a winner that will always win any challenges that I am confronted with.